Where do rainbows end?

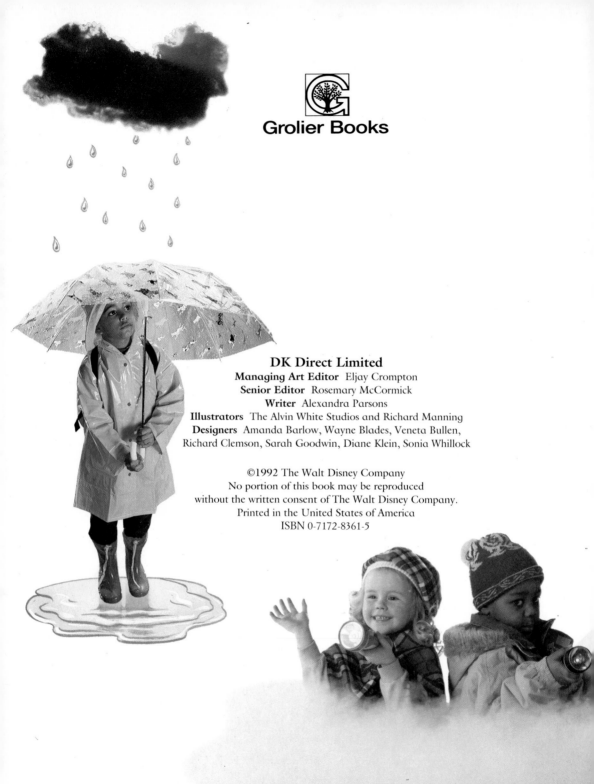

Grolier Books

DK Direct Limited
Managing Art Editor Eljay Crompton
Senior Editor Rosemary McCormick
Writer Alexandra Parsons
Illustrators The Alvin White Studios and Richard Manning
Designers Amanda Barlow, Wayne Blades, Veneta Bullen,
Richard Clemson, Sarah Goodwin, Diane Klein, Sonia Whillock

Contents

How do we know what the weather will be?

Because weather scientists have special equipment that can measure all sorts of things we can't see. Scientists can measure how much moisture there is in the air to find out if rain is coming. They have thermometers to tell how hot or cold it is. Even with all their equipment, sometimes scientists still get it wrong!

The modern way
Scientists also find out about clouds, storms, and wind speeds from weather satellites. They are special spacecraft which float around the earth taking photographs and collecting information about the weather.

5

Nature's way

☞ Long ago, people learned that nature gives a lot of clues about the weather. Take your umbrella if you see that pine cones are all closed up, or if cows are lying down in the fields.

☞ If the sky is red in the evening, and if crickets are chirping loudly, then don't forget your sunglasses.

What are thunder and lightning?

They are the sounds and sights of an electric storm. Inside a thundercloud very strong air currents throw ice crystals and water drops around and smash them together. This strong movement fills the crystals and drops with electricity. Electric sparks, or lightning, shoot through the cloud or flash to the ground. This makes the air so hot it pops like a bursting balloon - making thunder.

6

Take care!
Lightning that zig-zags to Earth is called fork lightning. It can be dangerous if it hits people, trees, or buildings.

Simply shocking
What did the thundercloud say to the lightning?
Don't be so flashy!

Crash, bang, flash facts

You can figure out how far away a storm is by counting the number of seconds between the lightning and thunder. Five seconds means a mile.

Where is rain before it falls?

It's in the clouds! It gets there because warm, moist air rises from the ground, and as it rises it cools and makes tiny water droplets. Clouds are lots of these water droplets gathered together. Sometimes, the little water droplets join up to become bigger raindrops. When the drops become too heavy to stay in the clouds they fall as rain.

8

Drippy rain facts

👉 Water rises into the air from oceans, lakes, and rivers.

👉 People, plants, and animals also give off moisture into the air.

👉 Water stays in the air for about 10 days before it falls again as rain or snow.

Black and white
Little fluffy clouds don't have much water in them so they look white. Big thick clouds are so full of raindrops they look black. That's because no light can shine through them.

Where do rainbows end?

They don't really end anywhere! In fact, if you were in a plane and looked down at a rainbow you'd see a circle of color. We see rainbows when the sun shines on falling raindrops. The raindrops reflect the sun's light – which is made of many wonderful colors. As the sunlight passes through the raindrops, it splits up into bands of color.

10

Beautiful colors
The colors of a rainbow are always in the same order – red, orange, yellow, green, blue, indigo, and violet.

Rainbow magic

☞ In Ireland people used to say there was a magic pot of gold at the end of every rainbow. But of course you can't find the end of a rainbow – so no one will ever know if it's true or not!

A colorful surprise
What kind of bow is impossible to tie?
A rainbow!

What is wind?

Wind is air moving. Sometimes it moves very slowly and we feel a nice, soft breeze. When it moves more quickly it can become a gale or even a hurricane. In the strongest winds, air is moving faster than a racing car!

Wind at work

People have learned to put the wind to work. In California, there are wind farms where thousands of wheels with blades on them spin around. This spinning energy from the wind is turned into electricity.

Wild, windy facts

☞ Winds are named for the direction they're coming from. So, a wind that comes from the east is called an easterly wind.

☞ Monsoons are winds in tropical places that change direction with the season.

What is a tornado?

It's a dangerous, fast-moving, swirling, funnel of wind. Tornadoes start inside huge thunderclouds, and then spinning air moves down from the center of the cloud to the ground. Tornadoes act like a giant vacuum cleaner, sucking things up from the ground and throwing them into the air.

Stormy facts

☞ Tornadoes can move as fast as 300 mph. Some have even moved as fast as 500 mph.

☞ Hurricanes begin as small thunderstorms over warm seas, then pick up speed. They can move as fast as 220 mph.

rricane watch

rricanes are
pical storms. They
different from
nadoes because the
ter of a hurricane, which
alled the "eye," is
n, but the outside part
ery dangerous.

Where does frost come from?

Frost is frozen dew. Dew is the little drops of water you sometimes see on leaves and grass. De freezes on cold nights when there are no clouds and no wind. If there were clouds they would act like a blanket, keeping the earth warm. If there were wind, warm and cold air would get mixed up, and it might not get cold enough to make frost.

16

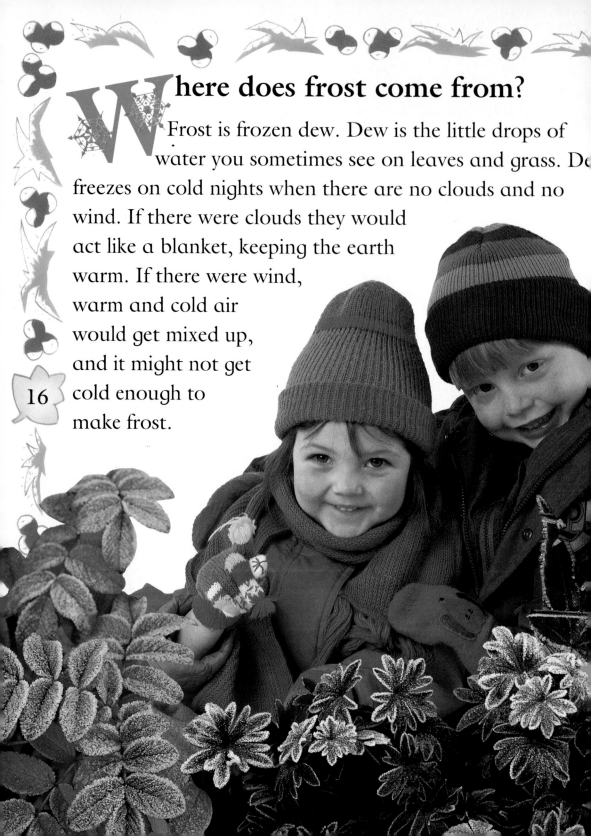

ck Frost

ng ago, a character called
ck Frost was thought to
n his icy fingers over
 world and make
st. But we know
tter!

Frosty patterns
The frost that
forms on misty
windows is called
fern frost.

Frosty facts

☞ Frost can form on airplane
wings while planes are
flying up high where the
air is cold. This can be
dangerous, so airplanes
have special equipment to
get rid of the ice.

☞ Long ago, the weather
was much colder in winter
than it is now. Rivers froze
solid, and people got
together and had markets
and fairs on the ice.

What is snow made of?

Crystals of ice. Water vapor in clouds freezes into ice crystals. If it is cold enough, the crystals will fall as snow. If it is not quite freezing, the snow crystals wi melt and fall as rain.

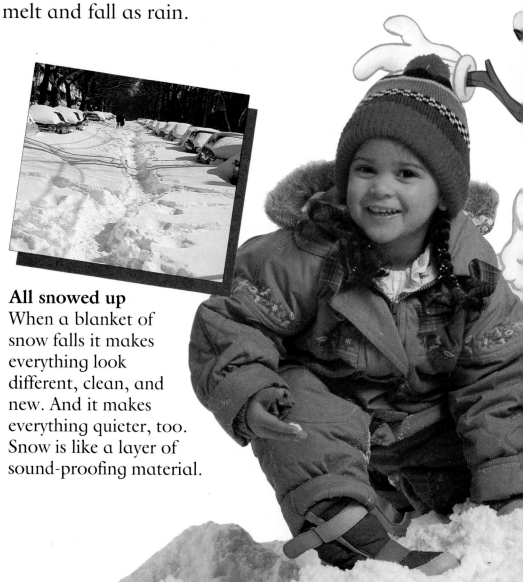

All snowed up
When a blanket of snow falls it makes everything look different, clean, and new. And it makes everything quieter, too. Snow is like a layer of sound-proofing material.

Pretty crystals

Snowflakes are made of flat crystals. If you looked at a snowflake under a microscope, you would see a six-sided crystal like this. No two snowflakes ever look the same.

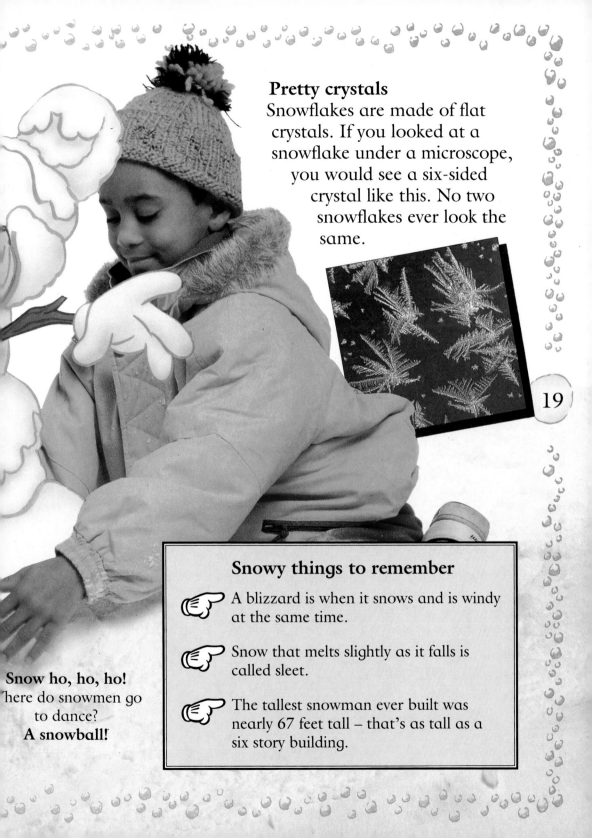

Snowy things to remember

☞ A blizzard is when it snows and is windy at the same time.

☞ Snow that melts slightly as it falls is called sleet.

☞ The tallest snowman ever built was nearly 67 feet tall – that's as tall as a six story building.

Snow ho, ho, ho!
here do snowmen go to dance?
A snowball!

How are icicles made?

They are made when the temperature falls a[nd] freezes drops of water and snow that had begu[n] to melt. Icy crystals form and stick to each other. Icicles [are] usually made on nights when it is very, very cold.

Icing icicles

In Germany, gingerbread houses are made at Christmastime. The walls are cookies, the windows are candy, and the icicles dripping off the roof are made of icing. These are the kind of icicles you SHOULD eat!

Frozen flow

Isn't this amazing? When it gets very, very, very cold, even fast-moving waterfalls freeze solid.

An icy story

Before refrigerators were invented, farmers used to flood their fields in winter and wait for the water to freeze and turn to ice. Then they cut the ice up into large chunks and took it to the towns. There it was stored in underground ice houses. Now all we have to do is open the refrigerator!

21

Why is the sky blue?

The answer to this question is a little tricky. Sunlight is made up of all the colors of the rainbow. But when it shines on the atmosphere (the thick blanket of air which surrounds the earth), gases in the air bounce mostly blue light toward our eyes.

Red sky at night
Sometimes the sky looks red. This happens when the sun is low in the sky and it shines through thick air. All the other colors get soaked up except for red.

Colorful sky facts

 In countries close to the north and south poles, spectacular colored lights can sometimes be seen in the sky.

 The air doesn't just stop where space begins. It slowly disappears the higher up you go, until there is no air left.

What is fog?

It is a cloud that is close to the ground. And a cloud is a mass of watery mist. Fog happens when very damp air settles close to the ground, and stays there. There is often fog early in the morning before the sun has had a chance to warm the damp air and make it rise.

Smoggy air
Smog happens when the air gets filled up with dust and soot and becomes thick and black and very unhealthy to breathe.

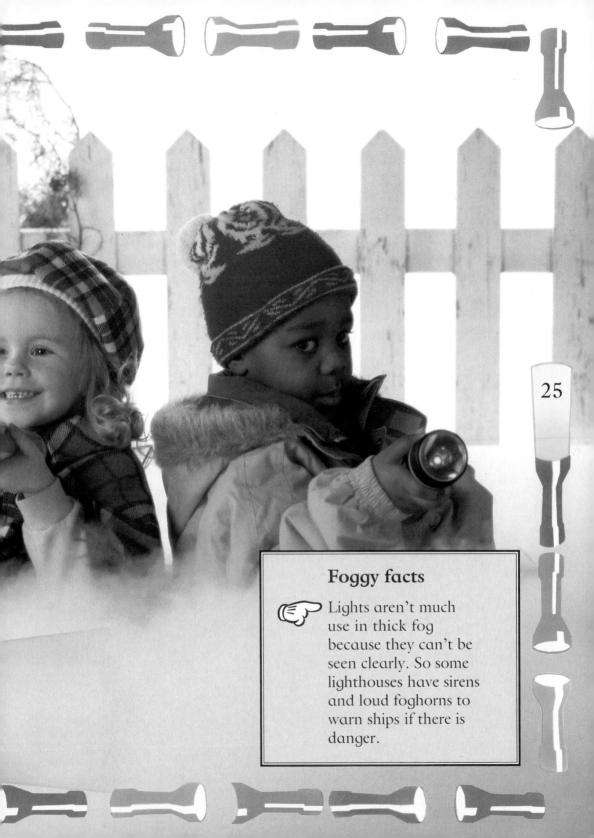

Foggy facts

Lights aren't much use in thick fog because they can't be seen clearly. So some lighthouses have sirens and loud foghorns to warn ships if there is danger.

What happens in a drought?

When it hasn't rained for a long time, the ground gets very dry. All the water that had collected in rivers, lakes, and reservoirs starts to dry up because heat from the sun causes it to rise as vapor. This is called evaporation. If the drought goes on for a long time, even underground water dries up.

No water, no food

A drought can be a serious problem for farmers. There is less drinking water for farm animals, and sometimes fields dry up and crops die.

Drought emergency!

☞ We need water for many things. But when there's a drought people are asked to help save water. Can you think of ways to use less water? Here are a few ideas to get you started:

☞ Don't leave the water running while you brush your teeth.

☞ Take quick showers instead of baths.

MICKEY'S Mind teaser

Only one of these rainbows shows the colors of a rainbow in the correct order. Do you know which one it is?

1

2

3

Answer: 2